W9-AJS-542

WITHDRAWN

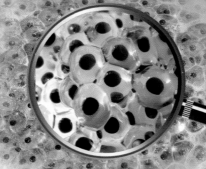

Growing and Changing

Let's Investigate Life Cycles

by Ruth Owen

Ruby Tuesday Books

Published in 2017 by Ruby Tuesday Books Ltd.

Editor: Mark J. Sachner
Designer: Emma Randall
Consultant: Judy Wearing, PhD, BEd
Production: John Lingham

Photo credits:
Alamy: 11 (bottom), 13, 15 (bottom), 25 (bottom), 27 (bottom); FLPA: 7 (bottom), 8 (top), 11 (top), 12, 14 (bottom), 15 (top), 16 (top), 18 (bottom), 19 (center), 20, 21 (center), 22 (top), 24, 29 (top); Getty Images: 9 (top), 19 (bottom), 27 (top); Nature Picture Library: 22 (bottom), 26 (bottom); Public Domain: 19 (top), 21 (top), 21 (bottom); Istock Photo: 5 (top); Shutterstock: Cover, 1, 2, 4, 5 (bottom), 6, 7 (top), 8 (bottom), 9 (bottom), 10, 14 (top), 16 (bottom), 17, 18 (top), 23, 25 (top), 26 (top), 28 (bottom), 29 (bottom), 30–31; Warren Photographic: 28 (top).

Library of Congress Control Number: 2016918440

ISBN 978-1-911341-31-4

Printed and published in the United States of America

For further information including rights and permissions requests, please contact our Customer Service Department at 877-337-8577.

Contents

Words shown in **bold** in the text are explained in the glossary.

The download button shows there are free worksheets or other resources available. Go to:

www.rubytuesdaybooks.com/getstarted

What Is a Life Cycle?

A life cycle is the story of how an animal grows and changes.

This is the story of a robin's life cycle.

A female robin collecting nest material

A male and female robin meet up and **mate**.

The female builds a nest from grass and twigs. She lays her eggs inside.

Egg

Nest

The female robin sits on the eggs to keep them warm.

After two weeks, chicks hatch from the eggs.

Chick

A newly hatched robin chick has no feathers, and it cannot see.

Let's Talk

What do you think the parent robins will do now?

Busy Parents

The parent robins work hard catching worms and **insects** for their chicks to eat.

Mother robin

Father robin

The chicks soon open their eyes and their feathers grow.

14-day-old chick

At 14 days old, the chicks leave the nest. They flutter around and learn to fly.

Young robins try out different foods to discover what is good to eat. They beg their mom and dad for food, too.

A chick lives with its parents until it is about six weeks old.

Father robin

Chick

At one year old, a robin is ready to have chicks of its own.

A New Family

All baby birds begin their lives by hatching from an egg.

Female swan

Nest

Male swan

A female swan lays her eggs in a huge nest of sticks and grass.

The parent swans take turns sitting on the eggs to keep them warm.

Eggs

This egg is life-size.

After about five weeks, the baby swans hatch from their eggs.

Baby swan

A baby swan is called a cygnet.

Cygnet

Growing and Changing

After just two days, the little cygnets are able to swim with their parents.

Cygnet

The cygnets are covered with fluffy, gray feathers called down.

Three-month-old cygnet

The cygnets get bigger and grow brown feathers.

Cygnets live with their parents until they are about five months old.

Five-month-old swan

At five months old, a young swan can fly and its white adult feathers are growing.

A swan becomes an adult when it is about three years old.

A Frog's Life Cycle

It's not only birds that begin their lives as eggs—frogs do, too!

Female frog

In spring, a female common frog lays up to 2,000 eggs in a pond.

Eggs

Each tiny black egg is inside a round blob of soft, clear jelly.

After several weeks, an egg becomes a tadpole that wriggles out of the jelly.

Jelly

A tadpole forming

Let's Talk

Why do you think frog eggs are inside jelly?
(The answer is at the bottom of the page.)

Tadpole

Tail

A tadpole can only breathe underwater. It uses body parts called **gills** to take in **oxygen** from the water.

Answer: The jelly sticks the eggs together and helps them float. It also keeps them from getting damaged. The jelly makes it more difficult for fish and other animals to quickly swallow the tiny eggs.

13

Tadpole to Froglet

A tadpole goes through lots of changes.

Tadpoles

Tadpoles eat slimy, green **algae** and tiny pond animals.

Algae

After about 16 weeks, a tadpole grows back legs.

Leg

Soon the tadpole's front legs grow.

Its tail gets shorter and shorter, until the tadpole no longer has a tail.

Front leg

As a tadpole changes into a frog, its lungs develop. Then it is able to breathe air.

Froglet

The tadpole becomes a tiny froglet that lives on land and in water.

A Froglet Grows Up

A froglet grows bigger and bigger until it becomes an adult frog.

Adult common frog

A frog lays eggs in a pond.

Let's Draw It!

Try telling the story of a frog's life cycle as a comic strip.

Draw the ways in which a tadpole changes to become an adult frog.

Use these words in your story:

- *tadpole*
- *front legs*
- *tail*
- *lungs*
- *eggs*
- *gills*
- *adult*
- *back legs*

A Frog's Life Cycle

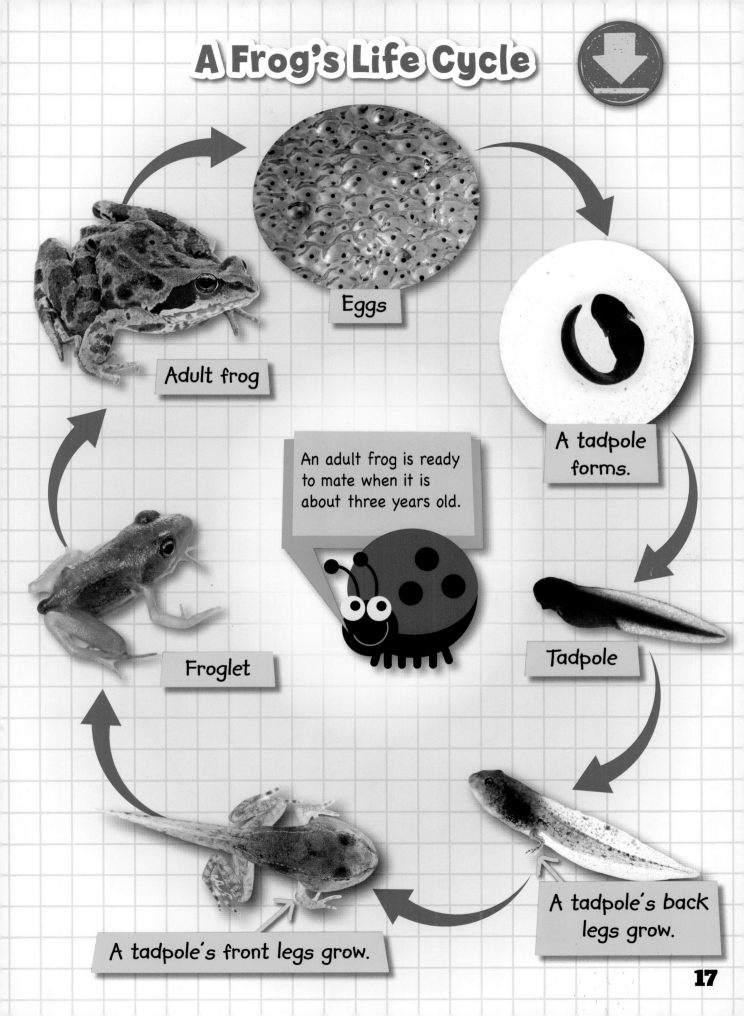

Eggs

A tadpole forms.

Adult frog

An adult frog is ready to mate when it is about three years old.

Froglet

Tadpole

A tadpole's back legs grow.

A tadpole's front legs grow.

An Insect's Life Cycle

The life cycles of insects, such as butterflies and bees, also begin with an egg.

A cabbage white butterfly lays up to 100 eggs.

Cabbage white butterfly

Egg

Tiny yellow caterpillars with shiny black heads hatch from the eggs.

Caterpillar

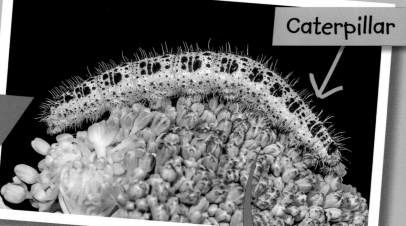

Caterpillar

As the caterpillar grows larger, it gets hairy with black splotches.

In the next stage of the insect's life, it becomes a **chrysalis** inside a case, or skin.

Chrysalis

Chrysalis case

Butterfly

While the insect is a chrysalis, it changes shape and grows wings.

It emerges from its chrysalis case as a butterfly.

A Bee's Life Cycle

Honeybees are insects that live in a home called a hive. Inside the hive are combs made up of tiny six-sided cells, or holes.

Worker bee

Queen bee

Cells

There may be 50,000 worker bees living in a hive. There is also one large queen bee.

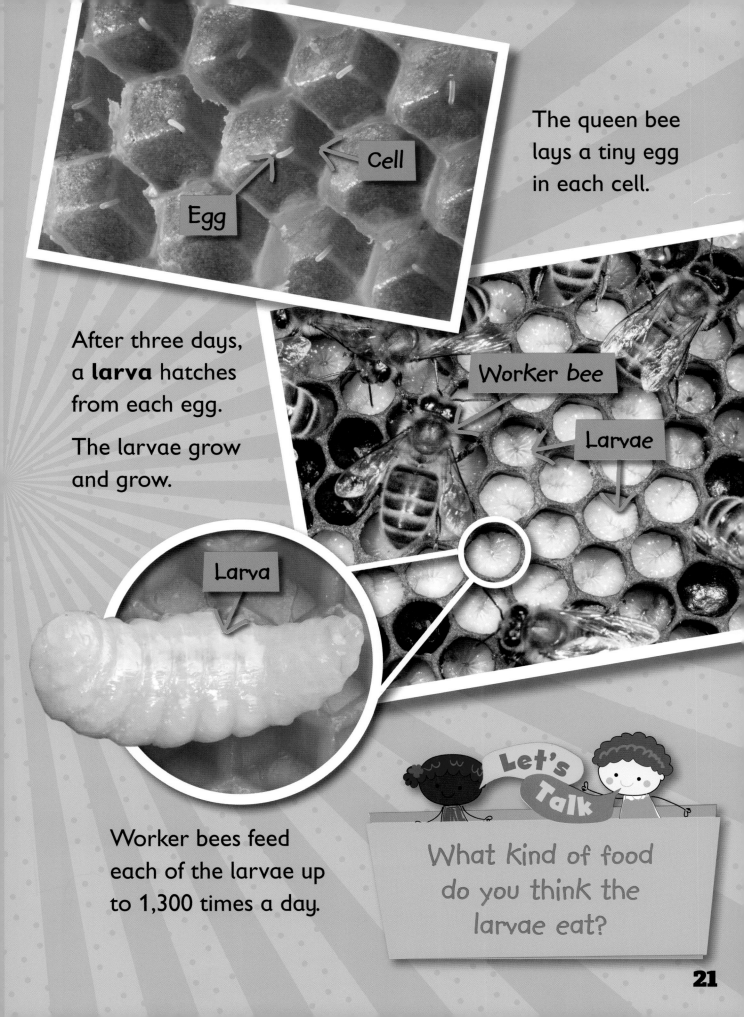

Cell

Egg

The queen bee
lays a tiny egg
in each cell.

After three days,
a **larva** hatches
from each egg.

The larvae grow
and grow.

Worker bee

Larvae

Larva

Worker bees feed
each of the larvae up
to 1,300 times a day.

Let's Talk

What kind of food
do you think the
larvae eat?

A New Honeybee

Inside its cell, a larva grows bigger and then becomes a **pupa**.

Pupa

It takes about 10 days for a pupa to develop into a honeybee.

A new honeybee climbs from its cell.

Worker honeybees visit flowers to collect **pollen** and a sweet liquid called nectar.

Back at the hive, workers make a food called bee bread from pollen and nectar.

The workers feed bee bread to the larvae.

Honeybees eat some nectar and turn some into honey. They store honey in the hive to eat in winter when there are no flowers around.

Pollen

Worker honeybee

A Sheep's Life

Animals such as sheep, cows, and dogs are **mammals**. A baby mammal grows inside its mother's body.

This sheep has just given birth to twin lambs.

She gently licks them clean.

Lamb

After just one hour, the lambs can stand and walk.

Mammals are animals with hair, fur, or wool. A mammal mother feeds her babies with milk from her body.

Mother sheep

Three-week-old lambs

Be a Scientist!

It's your turn to write the words!

What is happening in the pictures on this page?

How are the lambs changing?

Write a description of what you observe in each picture.

Mother sheep

Three-month-old lambs

Growing Up Fast

Not all baby mammals look like their mother when they are born.

Mother wood mouse

Entrance to nest

A wood mouse gives birth to her babies in an underground nest.

Baby wood mouse

A newborn baby wood mouse has no fur, and it cannot see.

After one week, the babies' fur starts to grow.

Seven-day-old wood mouse

At two weeks old, the babies' eyes have opened.

Two-week-old wood mouse

When the babies are three weeks old, they leave their mother and begin their grown-up life!

The Same and Different

The life cycles of mammals are similar in some ways and different in others.

A female dog gives birth to three, four, five—even 12 puppies.

Puppies drinking milk

A puppy cannot walk until it is about four weeks old. It becomes an adult at about two years old.

Adult

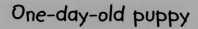

One-day-old puppy

Four-week-old puppy

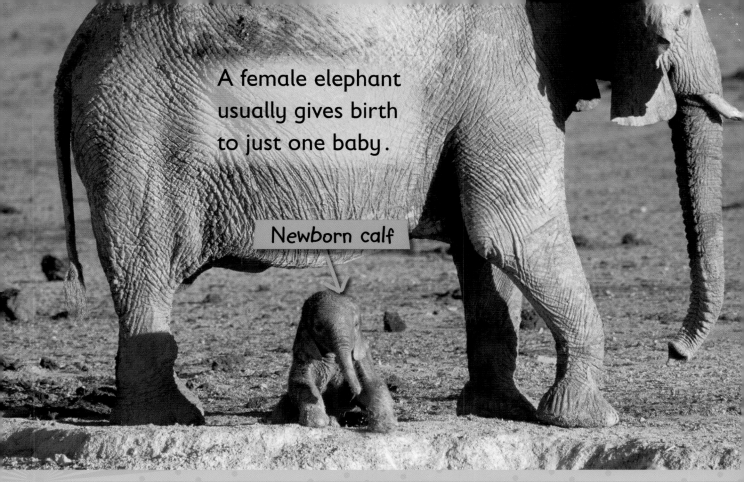

A female elephant usually gives birth to just one baby.

Newborn calf

The newborn elephant calf wobbles to its feet and can walk soon after it is born.

A calf drinking milk

An elephant doesn't become an adult until it's about 16 to 18 years old.

Your Life Cycle

Just like every other living thing, you have a life cycle. Your life cycle has five stages.

A

B

C

D

E

This woman is expecting a baby.

Check It Out!

These pictures show people at different life stages.

Can you put them in order from youngest to oldest?

Match these words to the pictures:
- **Older person**
- **Baby**
- **Teenager**
- **Adult**
- **Child**

(The answers are at the bottom of page 31.)

A baby needs help to live and grow. In what ways do adults take care of babies?

What things can you do now that you couldn't do when you were a baby?

How do adults take care of you?

How are your life and an adult's life similar and different?

Look at a picture of yourself as a baby.

How have you changed? In what ways are you still the same?

31

Glossary

algae (AL-gee)
Plant-like living things that mostly grow and live in water.

chrysalis (KRISS-uh-liss)
The stage in a butterfly or moth's life when it develops into an adult.

gills (GILZ)
Body parts that some animals use for breathing underwater. Fish and tadpoles have gills.

insect (IN-sekt)
An animal with six legs, a body in three sections, and a hard shell called an exoskeleton.

larva (LAR-vuh)
A young insect that looks like a fat worm.

mammal (MAM-uhl)
A warm-blooded animal with fur, hair, or wool. Mammals give birth to live babies and feed them milk.

mate (MATE)
To get together to produce young.

oxygen (OK-suh-juhn)
An invisible gas in air that living things need to breathe. There is also oxygen in water.

pollen (POL-uhn)
A colored dust that is made by flowers, and is needed for making seeds.

pupa (PYOO-puh)
The stage in the life of some insects when they develop into an adult.

Index